A New To[...]

Getting a new job u[...]
luck, timing, and pla[...]
have a dynamite resumé, you're not guaranteed a job
offer—or the salary you want.

But this book reveals a unique method for tipping
the scales in your favor. It explains how you can actually take one of the building blocks of the universe—
the vibration of energy—and make it work for your
career. The science of tracking these energy vibrations
is called numerology, and it's an invaluable aid for
calculating when you'll be most successful in different
phases of your job hunt.

Finally, here's an effective strategy to relieve the frustration of a long, drawn-out job search. Numerology
gives you the information you need to make sure that
the next step you take in your job hunt is the right one.

About the Author

Margaret Arnold is a retired librarian who lives outside Akron, Ohio. As a librarian she chose the metaphysical books for Stark County District Library in Canton, Ohio. She has studied numerology for many years and uses it to help others. She is interested in the study of the vibrations of time. She has been a Spiritualist for many years and is interested in many other areas of the study of vibrations.

Llewellyn's "How-To" Vanguard Series

How to Use Numerology for Career Success

❦ Margaret Arnold ❧

1996
Llewellyn Publications
St. Paul, MN 55164-0383, U.S.A.

FIRST EDITION
First Printing, 1996

Cover design by Llewellyn Art Department
Interior design and layout by Virginia Sutton
Editing by Darwin Holmstrom

Library of Congress Cataloging-in-Publication Data
Arnold, Margaret, 1952-
        How to use numerology for career success /
        Margaret Arnold—1st ed.
            p.   cm. — (Llewellyn's how-to series)
        Includes bibliographical references (p.)
        ISBN 1-56718-039-6 (pbk.)
        1. Numerology. 2. Fortune-telling by numbers.
3. Career development—Miscellanea. I. Title. II. Series.
BF1623.P9A67   1996
133.3'35--dc20   96-9054
                                                              CIP

Llewellyn Publications
A Division of Llewellyn Worldwide, Ltd.
St. Paul, Minnesota 55164-0383, U.S.A.

✦ Contents ✦

❧ 1 ❧

What Is Numerology?
What Are Vibrations?

Numerology is said to come from the teachings and calculations of the Greek philosopher Pythagoras, from whom the Pythagorean theorem also comes. He was a mathematical genius.

Numerology is a means of using numbers to depict vibrations. Vibrations are energy patterns. Numerology can be used to show the vibrations of people, the vibrations of a time period, or the vibrations of a person within a time period. The vibrations of time, not the vibrations of a person, are usually viewed in using numerology to look for work. This is because it is not likely you would know the vibrations of an interviewer unless the interviewer is previously known to you. Similarity in vibration does help during interviews, but because the interview is just a short period of time, the vibrations of the persons involved can generally be disregarded in the obtainment of a position. It is after people have been together for a period of time that the vibrations of the people will greatly affect their relationships.

The vibrations of time are important and most effective in using numerology to look for work. Because of that, for those just beginning to learn how to use numerology for the purpose of job hunting it is best just to learn about how to use the vibrations of time. Leave learning about the vibrations of people and the compatibility between the vibrations of people for later.

Numerology in Relationship to Job Hunting

To use numerology to find work, the vibrations of a person within a time period are viewed and analyzed. When numerology is used in job hunting, the numbers can tell when it is the best time to hunt. They cannot predict that you will get a certain job, but they can tell when to look for the best opportunities. The way it works is, if the right numbers are present, a better position, a more fitting position, a more pleasant position can show up. Without the right numbers, you might find a job, but the job will not be one of the better opportunities for you.

People should feel that there are better career opportunities for them. If they were aware of how to look at the right times, they would find it much easier to find better positions for themselves. Knowing how to use numerology to look for work helps you not miss opportunities. It also relieves the frustration of a long or ongoing serious job search. Knowing when to look means applying for the right jobs at the right time. It simplifies the search.

Numerology in Relationship to Career Success

Numerology can be used when you already have a position. When you have a position, you may want change. Sometimes you will want career advancement, a transfer, or just a different job at the same place. A knowledge of numerology can let you know when to seek whatever change you may want.

A knowledge of numerology can let you know when to seek work contacts socially and when it is time to actually ask for changes in your position at work. It can also let you know possible things that may happen in your present position. You can keep on top of the vibrational environment you are working under.

Steps for Learning How to Use Numerology to Look for Work

Some basic definitions are necessary for understanding numbers as they are used in numerology itself, and in using numerology to help you find work. This is just a beginning set of definitions. Other definitions will be added as they are needed, to help show how to use numerology to look for work.

Following the first set of basic definitions is a list of the characteristics of the numbers as they are used in numerology to find work and career success. The positive and negative aspect of each number will be given, plus its relationship to work.

Definitions

Main Nine Numbers

The **main nine numbers** in numerology are the numbers 1 to 9. These numbers represent different vibrations that correspond to characteristics of a personality, or to what may possibly happen during a period of time.

Master Numbers

The **master numbers** are 11, 22, and 33, and other numbers in this form, which are composed of the same double digit. These are numbers that represent a more intense vibration than the vibrations of the main nine numbers. The **master numbers** have the characteristic of standing alone. They are not broken down and added to other numbers. They may be combined with other numbers but are not usually reduced. Sometimes **master numbers** might be reduced to simplify understanding.

Simple Numbers

Simple numbers are the main nine numbers, as they stand alone, or the master numbers as they stand alone.

Compound Numbers

Compound numbers are the combining of the main nine numbers and master numbers—or the combining of master numbers with other master numbers. **Compound numbers** are written with commas between the elements of the number, to show all the elements of the number. **Compound numbers** are formed because master numbers are not broken down. Examples of compound numbers are **(11,2)**, **(11,5)**, **(22,1)**, **(22,3)** or **(22,6)**.

Work Numbers

Work numbers are those numbers under whose vibration it is a good time to look for work or make changes at work. The main **work numbers** are **1**, **4**, **8**, and **22**. **Work numbers** also include any simple or compound number that has one of the main work numbers in it, or that, if broken down, adds up to a work number. This is because both these types of numbers will have some of the characteristics of a main **work number**.

Included in this group are numbers such as **13**, **14**, **17**, **18**, **19**, **24**, **26**, **28**, **31** (all simple numbers found in the calendar). Also included are numbers like **(2,11)**, **(4,11)**, **(6,11)**, **(8,11)**, **(11,11)** (all forms of **22**), and other compounds in the same pattern.

On rare occasions a triple compound may show up. Examples of triple compounds are **(1,11,11)**, **(2,11,11)**, **(3,11,11)**, **(4,11,11)**, **(5,11,11)**, **(6,11,11)**, **(7,11,11)**, **(8,11,11)** or **(9,11,11)**. Finding a four-digit compound is an extremely rare event. As the chart is worked out, higher master numbers such as **22**, **33** or **44** will show up, mostly in compound number form. Any of these, if they contain a work number, can be considered a work number.

Descriptor Numbers

Descriptor numbers are numbers that are not work numbers by themselves, but can help describe a work number, a work vibration, a work situation, or the vibration of a time period. The main **descriptor numbers** are 2, 3, 5, 6, 7, 9, and 11. **Descriptor numbers** can be simple numbers or part of a compound number.

How Numbers are Added in Numerology

In adding numbers in numerology all numbers (except master numbers) are viewed as the equivalent of the digits, which compose the number. For example:

$1 = 1, \ 10 = 1 + 0 = 1, \ 100 = 1 + 0 + 0 = 1$.

The digits are added over and over until they can be reduced no further. This includes the **sums** of the digits. For example:

$654 = (6 + 5 + 4 = 15)$, then $(15 = 1 + 5 = 6)$, so, $(6 + 5 + 4 = 6)$.

Master numbers are exceptions to this general rule. Usually they stand alone—they are not broken down. There are a few times when they can be reduced to their lower vibration. One of these times is in subtration.

Use the practice addition that follows to see how numbers are added together in numerology. These examples show how numbers are reduced to their simplest form in numerology. Pay attention to what numbers are added together and what numbers stand alone in the examples.

Practice Addition in Numerology

Adding Main Nine Numbers to Main Nine Numbers

Use simple arithmetic to add main nine numbers and main nine numbers.

Example 1

$$2 + 5 + 8 + 4 = 19$$
$$19 = 1 + 9 = 10$$
$$10 = 1 + 0 = 1$$

Example 2

$$9 + 8 + 1 + 3 = 21$$
$$21 = 2 + 1 = 3$$

Adding Main Nine Numbers to Master Numbers

Add main nine numbers and master numbers by adding the main nine numbers to the other main nine numbers, and the master numbers to the other master numbers. They are written by simply putting a comma between them.

Example 1

$$6 + 7 + 22 = 13 + 22$$
$$13 + 22 = 1 + 3 + 22$$
$$1 + 3 + 22 = 4,22$$

Example 2

$$1 + 5 + 11 = 6 + 11$$
$$6 + 11 = 6,11$$

Adding Main Numbers to Compound Numbers

Add main nine numbers and compound numbers by adding together the main nine number and the main nine number part of the compound number.

Example 1

$$5 + 2 + 11,1 = 7 + 11,1$$
$$7 + 11,1 = 11,8$$

Example 2

$$7 + 3 + 22 = 1 + 22$$
$$1 + 22 = 22,1$$

Adding Master Numbers to Master Numbers

Use simple arithmetic to add master numbers to master numbers.

Example 1

$$11 + 11 + 22 = 11,11,22 \text{ (a form of the 44)}$$

Example 2

$$33 + 22 + 11 = 33,22,11 \text{ (a form of the 66)}$$

Adding Master Numbers to Compound Numbers

Add master numbers and compound numbers by adding together the master number to the master number **part** of the compound number.

Example 1

$$11 + 22,7 = 33,7$$

Example 2

$$22 + 11,1 + 11,2 = 44,3$$

Adding Compound Numbers to Compound Numbers

Add compound numbers and compound numbers by adding the main nine number **part** of the two compounds together, and the master number **part** of the two compound numbers together.

Example 1

22,3 + 11,7 = 33,1

Example 2

11,2 + 22,1 + 11,3 = 44,6

How to Subtract in Numerology

Subtracting is not a function usually taught in numerology. This might be because it is not often used. However, there is one place where subtraction is used in a numerology chart of time. Subtraction is used to find the attainment for each month.

Because subtraction is not often used in numerology there is a lack of practical information in the literature on this subject. This is especially true when the subtraction involves master or compound numbers.

Because it is easiest to understand, because the master numbers are often lived at their lower vibration, and because it lessens confusion, when subtraction is needed in the charts, read the master numbers as their lower vibration. See how this is done in the following examples.

Always subtract the lower number from the higher number, regardless of which number appears first. This often means that in subtracting, the master numbers are lower than the main nine numbers, since the master numbers are being read as their lower vibration.

Subtraction Examples

Subtracting Main Nine Numbers and Main Nine Numbers

Use simple arithmetic to subtract main nine numbers from main nine numbers. In numerology there are no negative numbers. If a negative number results from subtraction, drop the minus sign and use the positive form of the number.

Example 1

$9 - 8 = 1$

Example 2

$2 - 7 = 5$ (There are no negative numbers in numerology. Read all numbers in the positive form.)

Subtracting Main Nine Numbers and Master Numbers

If lived as a master number, this combination would not subtract, but for charting purposes reduce the master number to its lower vibration, then subtract.

Example 1

$11 - 9 = 2 - 9 = 7$

Example 2

$22 - 3 = 4 - 3 = 1$

Subtracting Main Nine Numbers and Compound Numbers

This can be done by subtracting the main nine number part of the compound number, or by reducing the compound to its lower vibration and subtracting the simple main nine number.

Example 1

$11,7 - 3 = (2 + 7) - 3 = 9 - 3 = 6$

Example 2

$7 - 22,6 = 7 - (22 + 6) = 7 - (4 + 6) = 7 - 1 = 6$

Subtracting Master Numbers and Master Numbers

Master numbers are subtracted from other master numbers by simple arithmetic.

Example 1

$11 - 22 = 2 - 4 = 2$ (or $11 - 22 = 11$)

Example 2

$33 - 22 = 6 - 4 = 2$ (or $33 - 22 = 11$)

Subtracting Master Numbers and Compound Numbers

When subtracting master numbers and compound numbers, more than one answer can be found. The compound number can be reduced, as far as possible, or the master number part of the compound can be subtracted with the simple master number.

Example 1

$11,5 - 11 = (11 + 5) - 2 = (2 + 5) - 2 = 7 - 2 = 5$

Example 2

$11 - 22,8 = 2 - (22 + 8) = 2 - (4 + 8) = 2 - 3 = 1$

Subtracting Compound Numbers and Compound Numbers

Subtract compound numbers from compound numbers by first reducing the compound numbers as far as possible.

Example 1

$11,3 - 22,5 = (11 + 3 = 2 + 3 = 5) - (22 + 5 = 4 + 5 = 9) = 5 - 9 = 4$

Example 2

$11,7 - 22,1 = (11 + 7 = 2 + 7 = 9) - (22 + 1 = 4 + 1 = 5) = 9 - 5 = 4$

❦ 2 ❦

Numeric Characteristics Relating to Time and Work

The One

Words to Describe the 1

1. Independent
2. Leadership
3. New beginnings
4. Alone
5. Boss
6. Initiator

The Positive Aspects of the 1

This is a time for a new start. New projects or new beginnings come with this number. Opportunities to take leadership may be presented. You may have to go it alone during this time, but there may be few interferences. This will be a time when you may have ambition and drive to push forward. It is a time that can bring much success, but you have to rely on your own self, not on others. At this time forge ahead. It is a good time for dealing with masculine energy. You will have to take control at this time and move ahead.

The Negative Aspects of the 1

This can be a time when you are too aggressive. You may appear to be domineering to others. During this time, you must not impose your will on others, and must realize that there is more than just self. The 1 can make a person boastful, impatient or arrogant. You may be pushy at this time and intolerant of others. Take time to think of others during the 1, so the negative selfishness of the 1 does not cause problems.

The 1 in Relationship to Finding Work and Career Success

The 1 is a **work number.** During your job search or career moves, definitely use this time. It is a time to look for new beginnings. The 1 has vibrations that will bring in new jobs or directions. The 1 may bring in work possibilities where you will be in a leadership position or have a new beginning. Get out and look for a position at this time. A positive 1 will give you the drive and push to look for work and to make changes in your life.

The types of jobs and ways to advance a career that you may find under the vibration of the 1 are numerous. You will find that these jobs will place you in the position of working alone, taking on a new beginning, or taking on leadership. You could become a boss in some way at this time. Teaching and leading others shows up under the 1.

The Two

Words to Describe the 2

1. Follower
2. Sensitive
3. Feminine
4. Diplomatic
5. Gentle
6. Little money

The Positive Aspects of the 2

The 2 is a quiet vibration, bringing a gentle quiet time. Under the 2, cooperation will be needed. You must work together with others and may be in a subservient position. You may help others put their ideas to use. The 2 vibration is a time for friendship and associations. It is a good time to deal with feminine energy and a very sensitive time. The 2 is not a vibration of work, but it may bring associations that help find work.

The Negative Aspect of the 2

You may have problems with associations at this time. You may feel shy or oversensitive when under the 2. The 2 does not bring confidence. This is not a material vibration, thus not a work vibration. Your physical health may not be at its peak.

Basically, the 2 is a time when you will want to be with others. It is a social type of vibration rather than a good vibration for finding work. Try to keep your confidence up during the 2 and keep trying. Do not be discouraged if there is a lack of money during the 2.

The 2 in Relationship to Finding Work and Career Success

As stated before, the 2 is not a work number, but it is

helpful to look at aspects of the 2 in relationship to the work numbers. A knowledge of the 2 and how it relates to the work numbers can help you understand the type of work that might show up when the 2 appears with a work number. Some numbers such as the 2 are descriptor numbers. They give an idea of the type of work to be found when they appear with a work number.

The 2, when found in relationship to work, indicates that you will be more of a follower than a leader. The 2 may be with a position where you must work in cooperation or association with others. It is also good for work of a religious nature or where inspiration is important. Work dealing with feminine energy is good under the 2 vibration.

The 2 is not a number where money is plentiful, so jobs found under this number may not pay as well as you would like. There may be other numbers, however, that will override this aspect of the 2. Always look at the entire group of numbers to get the best idea of what to expect under any vibration. Often work numbers will be included with nonwork numbers in a chart. Numbers should always be analyzed in relationship to the whole chart.

Usually the 2 is a good time to seek contacts for career advancement. This is a time just to get to know others. The 2 is a gentle number, so use it in a gentle way in getting to know others. Don't be pushy, just kind, gentle, and cooperative.

The Three

Words to Describe the 3

1. Happiness   2. Expression   3. Art
4. Friendship   5. Children   6. Pets

The Positive Aspects of the 3

By itself, the 3 is not a work vibration, but when the 3 appears with a work number it shows the possibility of a position or type of work that will be pleasant for the individual. It can generally be thought of as bringing the positive.

The 3 deals with self-expression and social interaction. It can mean friends or a friendly situation. It is a good number for public speaking or any type of public interaction. This is a good time to interview and make contacts.

The 3 is good for dealing with children and with animals, especially housepets. Companionship is also an aspect of this number.

The 3 can be a creative time. It is very good for inspiration, all types of creative jobs, and artistic expression. The 3 is generally looked upon as bringing pleasant experiences.

The Negative Aspect of the 3

By itself, the 3, as a vibration of time, does not have many negative aspects. It will probably be your own reaction to the characteristics of the 3 that might make it a negative time. For example, the 3 vibration will bring in things about self-expression, public speaking, children, pets, social interaction, creativity, or inspiration. You may not like public speaking, thus the 3 could be negative. Also, you may not like some of the other characteristics of the 3. This is how the 3 might become negative in relationship to work.

The 3 in Relationship to Finding Work and Career Success

The 3 is not a work number. Instead it is a descriptor: it helps show what type of position can be found during that time. Generally it will be work of a pleasant nature and may be concerned with any of the topics listed in the previous description of the characteristics of the 3.

During the 3, it is a good time to interview for a job, because it is a social vibration. It helps the interview go well, but it should be combined with or close in time to a work vibration to do this.

The 3 is a very good vibration to look for as a descriptor number when you are looking for a position. This is because it will bring in a type of work you might like rather than just a job. Specific areas of interests that are governed by the 3 are children, animals, artistic and other forms of expression.

The 3 is also good to use in seeking social contacts, if needed, in your present position. Usually it is a friendly time, so under the 3 do not hesitate to reach out. There are some exceptions to this aspect of the 3, but in general use the 3 as a contact time.

The Four

Words to Describe the 4

1. Material   2. Work   3. Order
4. Practical   5. Hard   6. Sturdy

The Positive Aspect of the 4

The 4 is one of the main work numbers. This is one of the main numbers to look for in a numerology chart when looking for times to job hunt or make changes in an existing job. Steady, secure work may show up during this time. It can bring stability, if lived positive. The key word with the number 4 is work. The 4 is the "down to earth" vibration. It brings in strength and practicality.

The Negative Aspect of the 4

One of the main negative aspects of the 4 is that it can bring hard times. There can be a harshness in personal relationships at this time. It is a very good time to interview, but because of the possible harshness in relationships you should be careful and approach interviews very positively at this time. The 4 might also bring a sense of restriction. A position where you might have to really apply yourself can show up under the 4. You may have to work hard.

The 4 in Relationship to Finding Work and Career Success

In relationship to finding a job or dealing with work, the 4 is one of the main vibrations to look for. In a job search it should be a very busy time. This is a good time to check the ads, to interview, or to scout around in search of work.

Under the 4 is usually a good time to call back on interviews, provided that you realize the employer may also be very busy at this time. Be tactful. Use the vibrations of each day. The 13th and 22nd of the month are good times for this, as they are forms of the 4, but they also have within them the aspects of the 2, the 3, or the 22. The 2, the 3, and the 22 are more social vibrations than a simple 4. They lessen the harshness of a simple 4.

When seeking work, the 4 is definitely a time to get out and try. In a job hunt, do not let this number pass by. As you use the 4, however, do not let the possible hardness of this vibration get in the way. Stay positive and responsive to those from whom you are seeking work.

The 4 can also be used for career changes or advancement. Changes in your present position may happen under the 4, but be careful when seeking changes under the 4. You have to remember to be very positive when under the 4 because the 4 can bring out a hardness in people.

The Five

Words to Describe the 5

1. Change   2. Travel   3. Temporary
4. Freedom   5. Visual   6. Sexual attraction

The Positive Aspect of the 5

The 5 vibration can bring positive change. The 5 can bring travel or adventure. It is a vibration of freedom and variety.

Under this number, things that happen are often of a temporary nature. This can be a positive number if change is accepted and used positively.

The 5 is also a very magnetic number. The sexes tend to attract one another under this number. You will look very good to those of the opposite sex at this time. Learn to use the attraction both in job hunting and in making changes in your existing position.

The Negative Aspect of the 5

The 5 can be one of the most positive of the numbers, or it can be one of the most problematic. The 5 can bring temporary situations when you really want permanent ones. It is also true that the attraction between the sexes must be watched carefully so there is no misuse of the sexual aspect of the 5. The variety, adventure, freedom, and travel aspect of the 5 could be negative in some situations.

Doing things in excess is sometimes considered a negative aspect of the 5. Usually, however, the 5 is uplifting.

The 5 in Relationship to Finding Work and Career Success

In relationship to finding work, the 5 can be both good and bad. Often, a job found under the 5 will be temporary. The fact that it will probably be temporary is the basic fact to remember about a position found under the 5, but remember that sometimes a temporary job will later develop into a permanent one. Sometimes the structure of the job itself will change, or sometimes a decision will be made to keep someone on after the temporary time limit has passed. Because of those reasons, you should not reject work just because it has been labeled temporary. Get all the facts about the individual situation first.

The 5 is very good for interviewing. This is especially true when interviewing with the opposite sex. It helps others to view you positively. The 5 day on which you are interviewed should be close enough to a day that has a work number vibration so that the decision about who gets the job is made during a time that you are under the work vibration.

If the 5 is being read as a descriptor number in a chart, the 5 is good for jobs pertaining to travel or ones that give more freedom than traditional nine-to-five jobs. If the 5 stands alone as just the characteristic of a time period, then the 5 is best used in a job search as an interview time or time to make contacts.

The 5 is good for making contacts to help you in career changes or career advancement. This is especially true when dealing with those of the opposite sex.

The Six

Words to Describe the 6

1. Love	2. Food	3. Domestic
4. Health	5. Music	6. Appearance

The Positive Aspect of the 6

As a vibration, the number 6 has many different positive possibilities. The 6 is a vibration that can bring confidence to those under its influence. It can also bring the need of service to others, and responsibility or adjustments. Under the 6 you may have to settle disputes, deal with home and family matters, or deal with appearance or health. Music is an area of interest also found under the 6.

With the confidence and responsibility it gives off, the 6 can quickly place you in a leadership position. Use the confidence that the 6 brings. Use the 6 for making friends, contacts, and looking good.

You must be able to adapt under the 6. Do not always look for perfection, as often happens under the 6.

The Negative Aspect of the 6

As positive as the 6 can be, so can it be negative. You may have problems in making adjustments and in accepting things as they are. A person under the 6 may seek perfection in everything around him or her. There may be problems in relationships, as you may tend to be argumentative. Usually under the 6 a person likes to argue as long as no one gets hurt, but often the receiver of the argument does not see it in that manner. The added confidence of the 6 may also bring difficulties in dealing with others.

The 6 also brings the problem of caring a great deal about what things look like. You may put too much value into appearances rather than looking at what is underneath. The 6 does help in letting you see what is really going on, but be careful, because appearances can be deceiving.

Health or domestic problems may show up under the 6. You must learn to serve at all different levels under the 6. Do not be domineering and attempt to force your will on others.

The 6 in Relationship to Finding Work and Career Success

The 6 is a modifying or descriptor number in a numerology chart for finding work. The 6 is not a work number that can stand alone in a numerology chart. This means that when the 6 is alone in a chart it does not depict a position, but when it is with a work number, it can give an idea of the type of job that is possible to be found. It may be work dealing with domestic type activities, clothing, cooking, health, art, or music. Jobs dealing with medicine fall under the 6. The 6 will usually bring in pleasant work.

The 6 vibration is good for all the health professions and for musicians. Restaurant work may show up under the 6. Whatever characteristic of the 6 is dominant, the service aspect of the 6 is also present. It can bring in assurance that there will be enough money as needed. The **6** also brings the possibility the personality will have to adjust. The vibration of the **6** provides positive energy for job interviews and enhances physical appearances.

Under the **6** is a good time to seek changes in your present position. You will look much better to those you work with at this time and come across as more knowledgeable, talented and confident. If you were afraid to ask for things before, this is the time to start speaking up.

The Seven

Words to Describe the 7

1. Alone   2. Wisdom   3. Perfectionism
4. Teaching   5. Chance   6. Scientific or religious

The Positive Aspect of the 7

The **7** is not a work number, but it affects any work number it is associated with. It is a number that brings a quiet and meditative vibration. This vibration is good for teaching, research, or religious pursuits. The **7** is not a material number.

Under the **7** you will spend much time alone. Jobs that call for you to be alone will fall under the **7**.

The Negative Aspect of the 7

There is a peculiar characteristic associated with the **7** in numerology. With the **7**, things have to happen by chance or when unexpected. Because of this aspect, when you are under the 7 it is best to try what you are attempting to do, even when at first it appears it may not succeed. Usually it will be the thing that you do not expect to succeed that will succeed when the 7 is present.

Under the 7, people have difficulty seeing things as they really are. You may misinterpret things that happen and things you hear.

The 7 in Relationship to Finding Work and Career Success

The 7 is a difficult number in a chart when the chart is being read for the purpose of finding work or seeking changes at work. The characteristic of unexpectedness is what makes the 7 difficult. That is because people do not apply for and attempt to get jobs they are not sure they have a good chance to get. The best approach to take when the 7 is in a chart with a work number is to try to find a job even if you feel you won't.

When the 7 is present, the type of work to be found can be quiet and studious. Teaching, religion, or research are found under the 7. There will be something about the job that will be unexpected.

It is also true that people do not usually seek job changes or job related advancements that they feel they may not get. Under the 7, just try. It will be that which you do not think will happen that will happen under the 7.

The 7 can also bring a delay in attaining a desired

position or in the actions necessary to obtain a position. You should not let this hold you back in a job search.

The Eight

Words to Describe the 8

1. Material   2. Money   3. Business
4. Authority   5. Courage   6. Hard

The Positive Aspect of the 8

The 8 is the number of power, authority, and material gain. It is a very material vibration and things of high quality can show up under the 8. The 8 is the number in which things are done in a big way. Advancement can come in money, achievement, power, or authority when you are under the number 8. If you want to step into power or authority, look for the 8 vibration.

The 8 gives confidence and a sense of power to those who are under it. Use this confidence as it comes. Much hard work can show up under the 8.

The Negative Aspect of the 8

As a number can bring positive aspects, so can it bring negative aspects. Instead of the positive accumulation of material things, a negative approach under the 8 can bring the absence of material possessions. The 8 can bring a lack of money and things. It can give a lack of power and success, giving much restriction. Under the 8 you will find yourself either on the top or on the bottom of where you are. If this number shows up as negative, it is best to just try to get through it, as vibrations change.

The 8 in Relationship to Finding Work and Career Success

In relationship to work, the 8 is a very good number. It is one of the main work numbers. When the 8 is present, it can mean a position of power and authority or a well-paying position. The 8 can also denote very hard work, power, and success. This is a very material vibration.

The 8 will give off confidence when looking for work. The 8 will give off an air of authority and competence. This is a very good time to job hunt.

In your job hunt do not let the 8 go by because this is one of the best vibrations to get a better position or find advancement in your existing position. A job found under the 8 will often be at a higher level than one found under the 4.

The Nine

Words to Describe the 9

1. Teaching
2. Travel
3. Humanitarian
4. Giving
5. Service
6. Kindness

The Positive Aspect of the 9

The 9 does not bring the vibrations of work but can modify a work number. On the positive side, the 9 is a number of humanitarian pursuits and it is a teaching number. The 9 gives a global outlook to things. It is also an understanding, intuitive and giving vibration.

The 9 will bring the urge to give or teach in some way. The 9 also makes you want to travel. Use the 9 as a number to get out and make contacts, network and make friends. The 9, if lived positively, will make you appear very positive and sociable to others.

The Negative Aspect of the 9

On the negative side, the 9 can bring highly charged emotions. It can also be as selfish as it can be giving. The 9 can depict the end or loss of something. When you are under the 9, be careful about this aspect of the vibration. Be careful that you are not ending something that you wish to continue.

The 9 in Relationship to Finding Work and Career Success

Even though the 9 is not a work number itself, it can be a very good time to interview. This is because of the giving and kindness aspect of this number. The 9 is also a very expressive number, so it is a good time for communication, such as in an interview. The **9** as a descriptor number can show humanitarian, teaching, travel, or ending qualities of a work vibration.

Use the **9** in your existing position. It is a vibration under which you can really reach out. Under the **9**, the kind and humanitarian qualities of your personality will show up.

The Master Numbers

The Eleven

Words to Describe the 11

1. Religious   2. Sharing   3. Inspirational
4. Theater   5. Aviation   6. Deep thinking

The Positive Aspect of the 11

The **11** is not a material number. It is just the opposite —the **11** is the number of intuition and inspiration. It may help in a job search or career advancement because of the added intuition it brings.

The **11** is a master number. This vibration is one in which idealism is very important. The **11** is considered the number of the "God force" and should be lived unselfishly. It is, when positive, a very giving and kind vibration.

Under the **11** you may have a more radiant personality. You may find yourself in the limelight.

The Negative Aspect of the 11

The 11 can be negative when it is handled wrong. The 11 is called the number of the "God force." Under the 11, the things of God, or the ways of doing things right, must be put first. Self-seeking under the 11 is what brings the negative. Be more than willing to give when you are under the 11.

Under the 11 you may be nervous, tense, and high-strung. You may have problems with confidence at this time. Be aware of the possible nervousness and confidence problem so you can be able to handle it. The 11 can be either the vibration of a leader, as it has the aspects of the number 1 in it, or it can be the vibration of a follower, because it is the higher vibration of 2.

The 11 in Relationship to Finding Work and Career Success

The 11, when positive, is a spiritual number. It is not a work number, but it may modify a work number.

The 11 is good for work dealing with religion or God. This vibration is good for positions where any type of inspiration is needed. When lived positive, the 11 brings in much inspiration and intuition. It is a vibration that is highly charged with nervous energy, a vibration where your personality will glow.

Work relating to electricity, aviation, and the stage often have, or are under, the vibration 11. Actors, pilots, and electricians are influenced by this vibration.

The obtaining of most jobs is enhanced when the 11 comes in conjunction with a work number. The inspiration of the 11 also helps in the interview process, if you are positive. During your job search do not forget the "God force" aspect of the 11 and live according to it. Be willing to help others in their job hunt as you look for yourself or try to advance yourself.

Remember to be a "giver" under the 11—under the 11, advancement or success will come from giving rather than taking.

The Twenty–two

Words to Describe the 22

1. Material   2. Groups   3. Humanitarian
4. Dominant   5. Work   6. Lacks confidence

The Positive Aspect of the 22

The 22 is an excellent work number. The 22 has within it the aspects of the 2, 4, and 11. This is a master number. It is the vibration of the master builder. The 22 is the number, under which building for humanity on a large scale is considered the ideal.

Because the 22 is a form of the 4, it will have many of the qualities of the 4. The 22, however, is much more expansive than the simple 4. It is more dominant, but usually not as harsh as the 4, because it has the 2 in it.

The Negative Aspect of the 22

As positive as the 22 can be, so can it be negative. The 22 carries within it all the possible negative qualities of the **2, 4,** or **11.** A negative **22** can bring very hard work or restriction. With the **22** having the **11** within it, it should be remembered the **11** is considered the number of the "God force" and be treated as such. This is not the time to be self-seeking.

Often, master numbers are lived as their lower vibrational equivalent. For the **22,** the lower vibration is the **4,** so all the negative aspects of the **4** could show up with the **22.**

The 22 in Relationship to Finding Work and Career Success

Under the **22,** excellent positions can be found. This vibration can be a very humanitarian vibration, which means it is good for any social welfare, humanitarian pursuits, or anything that deals with helping others on a large scale.

Social work positions fall under the **22,** as do health-related and religious positions. During this time your personal humanitarian or "people-helping" skills point toward the direction in which you should be looking for work. If you watch the vibrations carefully, you will see these are the types of positions that will show up.

Because of the element of the **2** and the **11** within the **22,** do not let this vibration pass by in your job search. The **22** is one of the best forms of the **4** to look for work under.

The **22** is also a social number. This means that it is both good for seeking work and seeking work changes. It can be a much more "softened" **4** than a simple **4.**

More Definitions

The following are definitions that are necessary for you to be able to read a numerology chart, as it relates to finding work. Included in this group is a chart of personal years, to make it easier for you to find your personal year, and then construct a chart for yourself. Following these definitions will be a sample chart. We will go over this chart step by step to show how it is read.

Attainments

The **attainments** are what can be achieved or attained under the vibrations of a particular month. The **attainments** for each month are found in the bottom triangle of the numerology chart for finding work and career success. These are positions **h, i,** and **j.** Look at the sample chart to see the placement of these positions.

Day Digit

The **day digit** is the date of a day reduced down as far as possible. A **day digit** may be one of the main nine numbers, or it may be a master number.

Week Digit

The **week digit** is the numerological number for the vibration of a specific week. It may be one of the main nine numbers, a master number, or a compound number. To find the **week digit** of the first 7 days of the month, add together the month digit and the personal year in the numerology chart for job hunting. This is position **a** and **b** added together. To find the second week (the **8th** to the **14th**), add together the personal year and third number in the base line of a numerology chart for job hunting. This is position **b** and **c**.

To find the third week (the **15th** to the **21st**, including the **21st**), add together the week digits for week **1** and week **2**. This is position **d** and **e** added together, which becomes position **f**.

To find the last part of the month, which is usually over a week (the **22nd** to the end of the month), add together the month digit and the third number in the base line. This is position **a** and **c** added together.

Month Digit

The **month digit** is the numerological number for the month. It is the number of the month reduced as far as possible. Use the following table for the **month digits**. The month of November is the only one that is a little complicated. The **11** of the number for November should also be checked as a **2**, because often the **11** is being lived at its lower vibration of **2**.

The following table shows the month digit for each month.

January = 1	July = 7
February = 2	August = 8
March = 3	September = 9
April = 4	October = 10 = (1+0) = 1
May = 5	November = 11 = (1+1) = 2 or 11 (master number)
June = 6	December = 12 = (1+2) = 3

Universal Year

The **universal year** is the numerological number for a particular year. It is found by adding together the digits of a year and then reducing them down as far as they can be reduced. Everyone is under the same universal year. The following list will show the universal year for some of the upcoming years.

$1997 = 1+9+9+7 = 26$ $26 = 2+6 = 8$
$1998 = 1+9+9+8 = 27$ $27 = 2+7 = 9$
$1999 = 1+9+9+9 = 28$ $28 = 2+8 = 10$
$$(10 = 1+0 = 1) = 1$$
$2000 = 2+0+0+0 = 2$
$2001 = 2+0+0+1 = 3$
$2002 = 2+0+0+2 = 4$
$2003 = 2+0+0+3 = 5$

Personal Year (definition and chart)

The **personal year** is the numerological number that indicates how a year will affect a person individually. To find the **personal year,** first find the universal year and add it to the person's month and day of birth. The month and day of birth should already be reduced as far as possible. For example, to find the **personal year** in 1999, for a person born August 18, 1952, follow these steps:

(1) Find the universal year for **1999. 1+9+9+9 = 28**
$$28 = 2+8 = 1$$

(2) Add the universal year to the month and birthday digit. The month and birthday digit should be already reduced.

1 (universal year) + 8 (month digit for August) + 9 (birthday digit) = **18**

18 = 1+8 = **9**

The **personal year** for a person born August 18, 1952, in the year 1999 is **9**. This person will have **9** as their personal year every **9** years.

❖ 3 ❖

Creating and Using a Chart

The following diagram shows a blank numerology chart for looking for work. This is the basic chart before anything has been filled in. This chart covers four months.

The next sample shows the different positions in a chart.

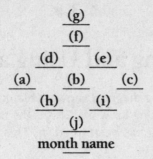

month name

The sample chart will be filled in step by step, position by position. First, the **base line** is filled in. The base line is positions **a**, **b**, and **c**, together. Begin with position **a**, which is the **month digit**. Its placement is shown in the following. If needed, reread the definition of the month digit. Remember that the number for each month is reduced to its lowest form in numerology. November can be read either as the master number, **11**, or the main number, **2**, depending on how it is being lived. In the sample chart, November will be shown as **11** in the base line, and when using addition, but when using subtraction, it will be reduced to **2**.

How to Use the Positions

a, b, c These 3 positions are the basic characteristics of the month

d, e, f, g These 4 positions are the characteristics of the weeks of the month

h, i, j   These 3 positions are the attainments. They
are what can be attained, obtained or felt
this month.

When using numerology to look for work, watch
for the work vibrations **1, 4, 8, or 22** in any of these
positions.

Position A

a 1 ___   ___ ___   a 2 ___   ___ ___

Jan.   Feb.

a 3 ___   ___ ___   a 4 ___   ___ ___

March   April

a = month digit

a 5 ____   ____ ____

May

a 6 ____   ____ ____

June

a 7 ____   ____ ____

July

a 8 ____   ____ ____

Aug.

a 9 ____   ____ ____

Sept.

a 1 ____   ____ ____

Oct.

a = month digit

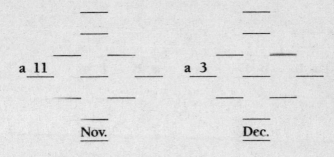

a = month digit

Position B

The next step is to fill in position **b** in the middle line. In this position, put the personal year of the individual that the chart is for. The personal year is found by adding the numerology digit of the birth month and day to the universal year. If needed, go back and review, how to find the personal year. In this particular chart, we will use a sample. Our sample will be for a person born August 19th. The chart will be for 2002.

Find the **personal year**.

8 (August) + **1** (19 reduced) + **4** (the universal year for 2002 = **13** (13 = 1 + 3) = **4**

4 is the **personal year** in 2002 for a person born August 19th. Place **4** in position **b** of the chart.

a_1___ b_4___ ____	a_2__ b_4__ ___
Jan.	Feb.
a_3__ b_4__ ___	a_4__ b_4__ ___
March	April
a_5__ b_4__ ___	a_6__ b_4__ ___
May	June

a = month digit
b = personal year

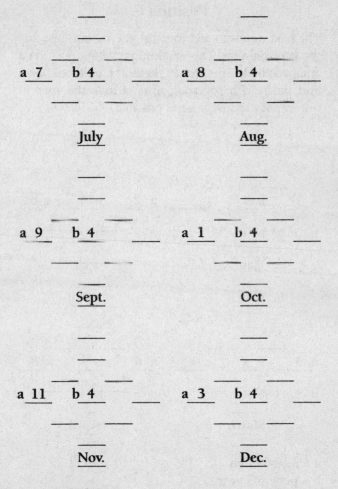

a = month digit
b = personal year

Position C

The next step is to add together the month digit and the personal year. This is adding together position **a** and position **b**. This creates position **c**. Add position **a** and position **b** together, and reduce the sum in numerology terms, as far as possible.

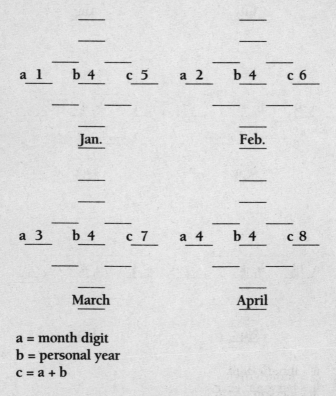

a 1   b 4   c 5   a 2   b 4   c 6

Jan.   Feb.

a 3   b 4   c 7   a 4   b 4   c 8

March   April

a = month digit
b = personal year
c = a + b

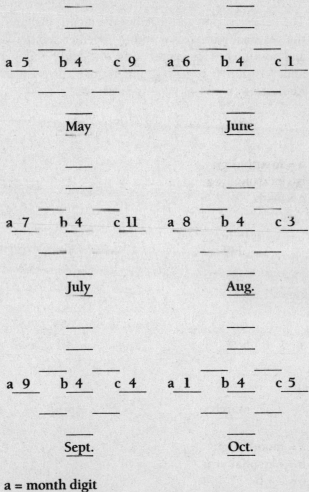

—			—		
—			—		
a 5	b 4	c 9	a 6	b 4	c 1
—	—		—	—	
	May			June	

—			—		
—			—		
a 7	b 4	c 11	a 8	b 4	c 3
—	—		—	—	
	July			Aug.	

—			—		
—			—		
a 9	b 4	c 4	a 1	b 4	c 5
—	—		—	—	
	Sept.			Oct.	

a = month digit
b = personal year
c = a + b

a 11	b 4	c 11,4	a 3	b 4	c 7

Nov.   Dec.

a = month digit
b = personal year
c = a + b

Position D

Position **d** is the vibrations of the first week of the month. Position **d** will show the characteristic of the first week, or what can be obtained during that week. It is day **1** through 7, including **7**. Position **d** is found by adding together position **a** and position **b** (the personal year and the month digit).

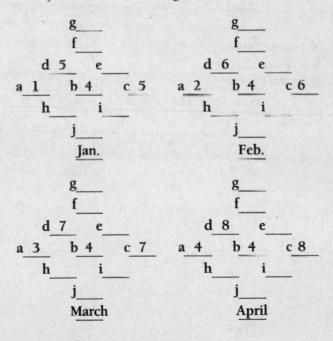

a = month digit   c = a + b
b = personal year   d = day 1 to 7

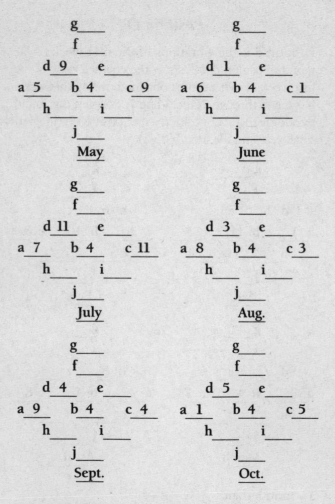

```
        g____                      g____
        f____                      f____
   d _9_    e____             d _1_    e____
a _5_    b _4_    c _9_    a _6_    b _4_    c _1_
   h____    i____             h____    i____
        j____                      j____
        May                        June


        g____                      g____
        f____                      f____
   d _11_   e____             d _3_    e____
a _7_    b _4_    c _11_   a _8_    b _4_    c _3_
   h____    i____             h____    i____
        j____                      j____
        July                       Aug.


        g____                      g____
        f____                      f____
   d _4_    e____             d _5_    e____
a _9_    b _4_    c _4_    a _1_    b _4_    c _5_
   h____    i____             h____    i____
        j____                      j____
        Sept.                      Oct.
```

a = month digit   c = a + b
b = personal year   d = day 1 to 7

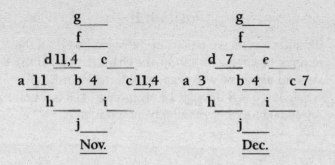

```
        g____                          g____
        f____                          f____
    d 11,4   c____              d 7    e____
a 11   b 4   c 11,4      a 3    b 4    c 7____
    h____   i____            h____   i____
        j____                    j____
        Nov.                        Dec.
```

a = month digit   c = a + b
b = personal year   d = day 1 to 7

Position E

Position **e** is the vibrations of the second week of the month. Position **e** will show the characteristics of the second week, or what can be obtained during that week. It is day **8** through **14**, including **14**. It is found by adding together position **b** and position **c**.

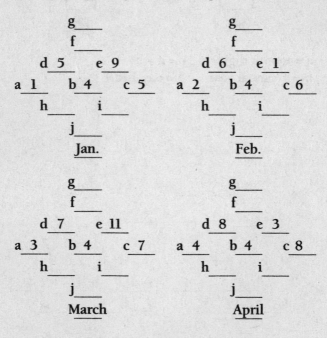

```
        g____                          g____
        f____                          f____
    d 5      e 9                    d 6      e 1
a 1      b 4      c 5          a 2      b 4      c 6
    h____    i____                  h____    i____
        j____                          j____
        Jan.                           Feb.


        g____                          g____
        f____                          f____
    d 7      e 11                   d 8      e 3
a 3      b 4      c 7          a 4      b 4      c 8
    h____    i____                  h____    i____
        j____                          j____
        March                          April
```

a = month digit   d = day 1 to 7
b = personal year   e = day 8 to 14
c = a + b

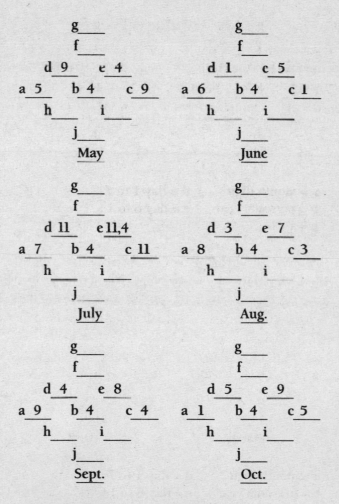

```
        g____                          g____
        f____                          f____
    d 9      e 4                   d 1      c 5
 a 5     b 4     c 9            a 6     b 4      c 1
    h____   i____                  h____   i____
       j____                          j____
        May                           June


        g____                          g____
        f____                          f____
    d 11     e 11,4                d 3      e 7
 a 7     b 4     c 11           a 8     b 4     c 3
    h____   i____                  h____   i____
       j____                          j____
        July                          Aug.


        g____                          g____
        f____                          f____
    d 4      e 8                   d 5      e 9
 a 9     b 4     c 4            a 1     b 4     c 5
    h____   i____                  h____   i____
       j____                          j____
        Sept.                         Oct.
```

a = month digit   d = day 1 to 7
b = personal year   e = day 8 to 14
c = a + b

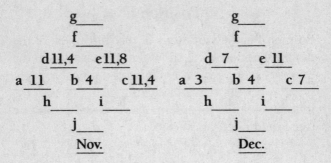

a = month digit   d = day 1 to 7
b = personal year   e = day 8 to 14
c = a + b

Position F

Position **f** is the vibrations of the third week of the month. Position **f** will show the characteristic of the third week, or what can be obtained during that week. It is day **15** through **21**, including **21**. Position f is found by adding together position **d** and position **e** (the first and second weeks).

```
        g___                        g___
        f 5                         f 7
    d 5      e 9              d 6       e 1
 a 1    b 4     c 5       a 2     b 4      c 6
    h___    i___             h___     i___
        j___                        j___
       Jan.                        Feb.


        g___                        g___
       f 11,7                       f 11
    d 7      e 11             d 8       e 3
 a 3    b 4     c 7       a 4     b 4      c 8
    h___    i___             h___     i___
        j___                        j___
      March                        April
```

a = month digit   d = day 1 to 7
b = personal year   e = day 8 to 14
c = a + b   f = day 15 to 21

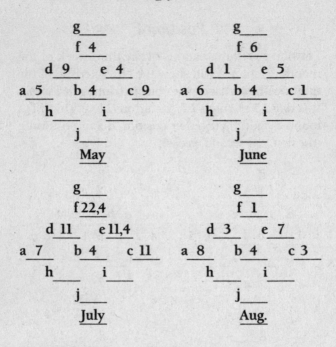

```
        g____                      g____
        f 4                        f 6
    d 9      e 4               d 1      e 5
a 5      b 4      c 9      a 6      b 4      c 1
   h____      i____           h____      i____
        j____                      j____
        May                        June


        g____                      g____
        f 22,4                     f 1
    d 11      e 11,4            d 3      e 7
a 7      b 4      c 11     a 8      b 4      c 3
   h____      i____           h____      i____
        j____                      j____
        July                       Aug.
```

a = month digit   d = day 1 to 7
b = personal year   e = day 8 to 14
c = a + b   f = day 15 to 21

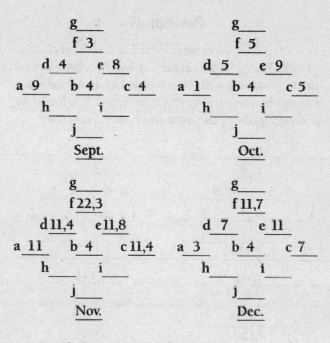

```
        g____                      g____
      f 3                        f 5
    d 4      e 8              d 5      e 9
  a 9    b 4    c 4        a 1    b 4    c 5
    h___    i___             h___    i___
        j___                      j___
        Sept.                     Oct.

        g____                      g____
      f 22,3                     f 11,7
    d 11,4   e 11,8            d 7      e 11
  a 11   b 4   c 11,4       a 3    b 4    c 7
    h___    i___             h___    i___
        j___                      j___
        Nov.                      Dec.
```

a = month digit   d = day 1 to 7
b = personal year   e = day 8 to 14
c = a + b   f = day 15 to 21

When reviewing the chart above, pay close attention to the month of November, as it is the **11th** vibration, which is a master number. The **11** can be added to other master numbers, but not to the **9** main numbers. Position **f**, in this case, can be written **22,9** or **11,11,9**. When analyzing a chart, look at all the possibilities.

Position G

Position **g** is the vibrations of the **22nd** to the end of the month. Except for February, it will be a little over a week. Position **g** will show the characteristic and what can be obtained during this time period. It is found by adding together position **a** and **c** on the baseline.

```
        g 6                      g 8
        f 5                      f 7
    d 5      e 9             d 6      e 1
 a 1     b 4     c 5      a 2     b 4     c 6
    h        i               h        i
       j                        j
      Jan.                     Feb.


        g 1                      g 3
        f 11,7                   f 11
    d 7      e 11            d 8      e 3
 a 3     b 4     c 7      a 4     b 4     c 8
    h        i               h        i
       j                        j
     March                     April
```

a = month digit   e = day 8 to 14
b = personal year   f = day 15 to 21
c = a + b   g = day 22 to month's end
d = day 1 to 7

```
        g 5                    g 7
        f 4                    f 6
    d 9      e 4           d 1      e 5
a 5     b 4     c 9     a 6     b 4     c 1
    h        i             h        i
        j                      j
       May                    June


       g 11,7                 g 11
       f 22,4                 f 1
    d 11     e 11,4        d 3      e 7
a 7     b 4     c 11    a 8     b 4     c 3
    h        i             h        i
        j                      j
       July                   Aug.
```

a = month digit   e = day 8 to 14
b = personal year   f = day 15 to 21
c = a + b   g = day 22 to month's end
d = day 1 to 7

```
              g  4                        g  6
              f  3                        f  5
        d  4      e  8              d  5      e  9
    a  9    b  4    c  4        a  1    b  4    c  5
       h___   i___                 h___   i___
          j___                        j___
         Sept.                        Oct.


              g 22,4                     g  1
              f 22,3                     f 11,7
        d 11,4    e 11,8           d  7      e 11
    a  11   b  4   c 11,4       a  3    b  4    c  7
       h___   i___                 h___   i___
          j___                        j___
         Nov.                        Dec.
```

a = month digit   e = day 8 to 14
b = personal year   f = day 15 to 21
c = a + b   g = day 22 to month's end
d = day 1 to 7

The Attainments

The bottom part of the numerology chart for finding work is called the **attainments** for the month. This part of the chart is created differently from the top part. Instead of adding together different positions, they are subtracted. Note: reduce master numbers to their lower vibration when subtracting them with any other type of number. They can be left as master numbers when a master number is subtracted from a master number. Appendix C lists what can be attained.

Position H

Position **h** is the first minor attainment for the month. It is found by subtracting position **a** and position **b**. Subtract whichever number is smaller from the number that is larger.

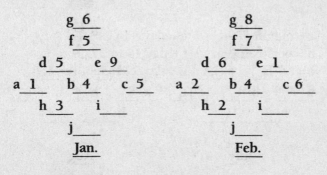

a = month digit   e = day 8 to 14
b = personal year   f = day 15 to 21
c = a + b   g = day 22 to month's end
d = day 1 to 7   h = minor attainment

```
        g 1                      g 3
        f 11,7                   f 11
    d 7      e 11            d 8      e 3
a 3      b 4      c 7    a 4      b 4      c 8
    h 1      i               h 0      i
        j                        j
       March                    April


        g 5                      g 7
        f 4                      f 6
    d 9      e 4            d 1      e 5
a 5      b 4      c 9    a 6      b 4      c 1
    h 1      i               h 2      i
        j                        j
        May                     June


        g 11,7                   g 11
        f 22,4                   f 1
    d 11     e 11,4         d 3      e 7
a 7      b 4      c 11   a 8      b 4      c 3
    h 3      i               h 4      i
        j                        j
        July                    Aug.
```

a = month digit   e = day 8 to 14
b = personal year   f = day 15 to 21
c = a + b   g = day 22 to month's end
d = day 1 to 7   h = minor attainment

g 4   g 6

f 3   f 5

d 4   e 8   d 5   e 9

a 9   b 4   c 4   a 1   b 4   c 5

h 5   i   h 3   i

j   j

Sept.   Oct.

g 22,4   g 1

f 22,3   f 11,7

d 11,4   e 11,8   d 7   e 11

a 11   b 4   c 11,4   a 3   b 4   c 7

h 2   i   h 1   i

j   j

Nov.   Dec.

a = month digit   e = day 8 to 14
b = personal year   f = day 15 to 21
c = a + b   g = day 22 to month's end
d = day 1 to 7   h = minor attainment

Position I

Position **i** is the second minor attainment for the month. It is found by subtracting position **b** and position **c**. Subtract whichever number is smaller from the number that is larger. In the sample charts below, November will be reduced to the lower vibration of **2** for ease in subtraction.

	g 6				**g 8**	
	f 5				**f 7**	
d 5		**e 9**		**d 6**		**e 1**
a 1	**b 4**	**c 5**		**a 2**	**b 4**	**c 6**
h 3		**i 1**		**h 2**		**i 2**
	j___				**j___**	
	Jan.				**Feb.**	

	g 1				**g 3**	
	f 11,7				**f 11**	
d 7		**e 11**		**d 8**		**e 3**
a 3	**b 4**	**c 7**		**a 4**	**b 4**	**c 8**
h 1		**i 3**		**h 0**		**i 4**
	j___				**j___**	
	March				**April**	

a = month digit	**f = day 15 to 21**
b = personal year	**g = day 22 to month's end**
c = a + b	**h = minor attainment**
d = day 1 to 7	**i = minor attainment**
e = day 8 to 14	

```
            g 5                             g 7
            f 4                             f 6
      d 9        e 4                  d 1        e 5
  a 5      b 4      c 9          a 6      b 4      c 1
      h 1        i 5                  h 2        i 3
            j____                           j____
           May                             June


          g 11,7                           g 11
          f 22,4                           f 1
      d 11       e 11,4               d 3        e 7
  a 7      b 4      c 11         a 8      b 4      c 3
      h 3        i 2                  h 4        i 1
            j____                           j____
           July                            Aug.
```

a = month digit   f = day 15 to 21
b = personal year   g = day 22 to month's end
c = a + b   h = minor attainment
d = day 1 to 7   i = minor attainment
e = day 8 to 14

```
              g 4                        g 6
              f 3                        f 5
        d 4       e 8              d 5       e 9
   a 9      b 4      c 4      a 1      b 4      c 5
        h 5       i 0              h 3       i 1
              j___                       j___
             Sept.                      Oct.


             g 22,4                      g 1
             f 22,3                      f 11,7
       d 11,4     e 11,8           d 7       e 11
  a 11      b 4     c 11,4     a 3      b 4      c 7
        h 2       i 2              h 1       i 3
              j___                       j___
             Nov.                       Dec.
```

a = month digit   f = day 15 to 21
b = personal year   g = day 22 to month's end
c = a + b   h = minor attainment
d = day 1 to 7   i = minor attainment
e = day 8 to 14

Position J

Position **j** is the main attainment for the month. It is found by subtracting position **h** and position **i**, the two minor attainments. Subtract whichever number is smaller from the larger.

<pre>
        g 6   g 8
        f 5   f 7
    d 5   e 9   d 6   e 1
 a 1   b 4   c 5   a 2   b 4   c 6
    h 3   i 1   h 2   i 2
        j 2   j 0
       Jan.   Feb.

        g 1   g 3
        f 11,7   f 11
    d 7   e 11   d 8   e 3
 a 3   b 4   c 7   a 4   b 4   c 8
    h 1   i 3   h 0   i 4
        j 2   j 4
       March   April
</pre>

a = month digit   f = day 15 to 21
b = personal year   g = day 22 to month's end
c = a + b   h = minor attainment
d = day 1 to 7   i = minor attainment
e = day 8 to 14   j = major attainment

g 5	g 7
f 4	f 6
d 9 e 4	d 1 e 5
a 5 b 4 c 9	a 6 b 4 c 1
h 1 i 5	h 2 i 3
j 4	j 1
May	June

g 11,7	g 11
f 22,4	f 1
d 11 e 11,4	d 3 e 7
a 7 b 4 c 11	a 8 b 4 c 3
h 3 i 2	h 4 i 1
j 1	j 3
July	Aug.

a = month digit   f = day 15 to 21
b = personal year   g = day 22 to month's end
c = a + b   h = minor attainment
d = day 1 to 7   i = minor attainment
e = day 8 to 14   j = major attainment

g 4
f 3
d 4 e 8
a 9 b 4 c 4
h 5 i 0
j 5
Sept.

g 6
f 5
d 5 e 9
a 1 b 4 c 5
h 3 i 1
j 2
Oct.

g 22,4
f 22,3
d 11,4 e 11,8
a 11 b 4 c 11,4
h 2 i 2
j 0
Nov.

g 1
f 11,7
d 7 e 11
a 3 b 4 c 7
h 1 i 3
j 2
Dec.

a = month digit	**f = day 15 to 21**
b = personal year	**g = day 22 to month's end**
c = a + b	**h = minor attainment**
d = day 1 to 7	**i = minor attainment**
e = day 8 to 14	**j = major attainment**

When you are learning how to use numerology to look for jobs, work with your chart. Pay attention to what happens each week. The patterns will begin to become evident. Whenever a compound number is in the chart, remember that the compound has within it the characteristics of all the numbers that make it up.

Using Day Digits

This is how to use a numerology chart to tell the vibrations of when to look for work on a weekly and monthly basis. It is also useful and important to know how to use day to day vibrations in a job search. This is the use of the **day digit.** The day digit is the numerological equivalent to the number of each day of the month. The number of the day is reduced, as far as possible, in numerology terms.

Recheck the definitions for each number, to see which numbers are good for looking for work. Some days are better for interviewing than others. Some days are better for finding work or seeking career success than others.

Remember the basic work numbers are **1, 4, 8,** and **22.** When reading a calendar, look for all variations and possibilities of these numbers, including those that have just one digit of those numbers. Included should be the **1st, 4th, 8th, 10th, 13th, 14th, 17th, 18th, 19th, 22nd, 24th, 26th, 28th,** and the **31st.**

For interviewing, remember that you do not necessarily get the job on the day interviewed. Sometimes days with more social vibrations are better for interviewing than actual work days. Just make sure to check back, and do employment ad checking on work days.

The more social vibrations are the **2nd, 3rd, 5th, 6th, 9th, 11th, 22nd,** and any day that may be a variation of or have the element of these vibrations. On a calendar, these vibrations would include the **2nd, 3rd,**

5th, 6th, 9th, 11th, 12th, 13th, 14th, 15th, 16th, 18th, 20th, 21st, 22nd, 23rd, 24th, 25th, 26th, 27th, 29th, 30th, and **31st.** These days are good for interviewing, even though some are not work days.

Look at the characteristic of each day to see how it relates to job hunting. The basic characteristics are listed below.

1st. This is a work day, good for new beginnings and independence.

2nd. This is not a work day, but might be good for interviewing or making job contacts.

3rd. This is a friendly day that might be good for interviewing or being social in an existing position.

4th. This is one of the best work days, but has a harsh quality, so be careful interviewing this day.

5th. This is a good interviewing day, especially with the opposite sex. It is also good for being social in your present job.

6th. This is a good interviewing day because things will look good, and the **6** brings confidence. Use the **6th** also to look good in your present position.

7th. Things have to happen by chance under the 7. It is not a good work day, nor is it good for interviewing.

8th. A very good day for work. It is the vibration of money, power, and authority.

9th. Not a good work day, but very social and can bring good feelings between people.

10th. This is a good work day, with the same characteristics as the **1st.** There is the possibility for leadership on this day.

11th. This vibration can be very kind and giving, which makes it good for interviewing. In an existing position, show your kindness on this day.

12th. This vibration is a form of the **3**, which makes it good for interviewing or making social contacts.

13th. This is a good work day and can be good for interviewing, because of the **3** and the overall **4**. Making social contacts may be worthwhile on this day, but don't let the harshness of the **4** take over.

14th. This is sometimes a good work day and sometimes a good day for interviewing or being social. The **4** might bring a harshness.

15th. This is a very good day for interviewing or for looking good in a present position because of the **5** and the overall **6**.

16th. The overall **7** of this vibration forces things to happen by chance. The element of the **6** might help in interviewing.

17th. Because of the element of the **7**, things have to happen by chance, but the overall **8** can make it a good work day. It can bring power and authority by chance.

18th. This day is good for interviewing and has a lot of work vibration. Be social on this day, whether looking for work or seeking changes in an existing position. Reach out.

19th. This day has the same characteristics as the **1st,** but it might be a little more social because of the **9**. This is a work day.

20th. This is a good day for interviewing, but not a good work day. Reach out gently on this day.

21st. This day has the same elements as the **3rd**. It is social and good for interviewing.

22nd. This is a good day for finding work or making changes in your present position, because it is both a social number and a good work number.

23rd. A very social day, good for interviewing and making contacts.

24th. This is a good interviewing day and it is social. It has the element of the **4**, a good work number.

25th. This has the overall vibration of **7** so things have to happen by chance here.

26th. This is a very good work day because of the overall **8**, and it's social, too, because of the **2** and the **6**.

27th. This might be a good interview or social day, but because of the **7**, things have to happen by chance.

28th. This is a good work number. It has the characteristics of the **1**, but is gentler, because of the element of the **2**.

29th. This day has the characteristics of the **11** or of the **2**. It can be good for interviewing, or it can help you to give selflessly in a present position.

30th. This is a good social day, good for interviewing. Reach out on this day in your existing job.

31st. This day can be both good for interviewing and good for looking for work. It can also be very good for seeking changes in your present position. Just don't let the aspect of the **4** become too harsh.

❧ Conclusion ❧

The value of learning how to use numerology to look for work is evident in the way it can help in a job search. Knowing the best time to interview and when better jobs will appear or manifest helps in looking for work and in building a career. It eliminates wasted time, and lessens frustration and effort in looking for work.

Numerology is also of value after one has obtained a position or begun a career. It can be used to help make that career a success. The knowledge of numerology can let you know when to seek advancement in your position or career. By following the work numbers, you can know when to move around in your career and when to seek advancement in your career. You can seek those changes at the right time.

The way it works is that the right vibrations for what you are trying to accomplish have to be there. Vibrations can not guarantee a job, a move, or a raise, but without the right vibrations, these things will not come.

Another reason to learn how to use numerology to look for work is to gain a deeper understanding and appreciation of life. Numerology shows that there is something behind what we see. It shows that an intelligence beyond our comprehension—some people say an infinite intelligence—is behind the thing we call life. This intelligence is what is called "God," or names meaning the same as "God," depending on the culture. This intelligence is viewed in many forms (some cultures view it as formless), but the vastness of that intelligence should be evident, regardless of the cultural concept of "God."

If you work with numerology long enough, even if it is in just one area, such as looking for work, you will find that only an intelligence beyond comprehension could have put together such amazing workings of vibrations. This intelligence made things in a way that allows these vibrations to be expressed by numbers. Even a daily, often materialistic activity, such as looking for work, is affected and often altered by vibrations. Understanding vibrations through numerology can help prove that there is a God.

Appendices

The following pages of appendices will show how each personal year should look in a numerological career chart. These charts are for personal years with simple numbers. There are personal years with compound numbers, but because there are so many variations on compound numbers, only the simple number personal years are shown. If you have a compound number as your personal year, convert the compound number to a simple number. This will give the vibrations of the year close enough to be able to understand the basic essence of the vibrations of the time period.

In these charts, when doing subtraction to find the attainments for each month, if master numbers and numbers other than master numbers are being subtracted from each other, the master numbers will first be reduced to their lower vibration. Negative numbers will also be changed to their positive form, for easy understanding of the charts.

❈ Appendix A ❈

Personal Year 1

```
        g  3                        g  5
        f  5                        f  7
    d  2      e  3              d  3      e  4
a  1    b  1    c  2        a  2    b  1    c  3
    h  0      i  1              h  1      i  2
        j  0                        j  1
        Jan.                       Feb.
```

```
        g  7                        g  9
        f  9                        f  11
    d  4      e  5              d  5      e  6
a  3    b  1    c  4        a  4    b  1    c  5
    h  2      i  3              h  3      i  4
        j  1                        j  1
       March                       April
```

a = month digit   f = day 15 to 21
b = personal year   g = day 22 to month's end
c = a + b   h = minor attainment
d = day 1 to 7   i = minor attainment
e = day 8 to 14   j = major attainment

```
        g 11                      g 4
        f 4                       f 6
    d 6      e 7              d 7      e 8
a 5     b 1     c 6       a 6     b 1     c 7
    h 4      i 5              h 5      i 6
        j 1                       j 1
        May                      June


        g 6                      g 8
        f 8                       f 1
    d 8      e 9              d 9      e 1
a 7     b 1     c 8       a 8     b 1     c 9
    h 6      i 7              h 7      i 8
        j 1                       j 1
        July                     Aug.
```

a = month digit   f = day 15 to 21
b = personal year   g = day 22 to month's end
c = a + b   h = minor attainment
d = day 1 to 7   i = minor attainment
e = day 8 to 14   j = major attainment

g 1
f 3
d 1   e 2
a 9   b 1   c 1
h 8   i 0
j 8
Sept.

g 3
f 5
d 2   e 3
a 1   b 1   c 2
h 0   i 1
j 1
Oct.

g 22,1
f 22,3
d 11,1   e 11,2
a 11   b 1   c 11,1
h 1   i 2
j 1
Nov.

g 7
f 9
d 4   e 5
a 3   b 1   c 4
h 2   i 3
j 1
Dec.

a = month digit   f = day 15 to 21
b = personal year   g = day 22 to month's end
c = a + b   h = minor attainment
d = day 1 to 7   i = minor attainment
e = day 8 to 14   j = major attainment

Personal Year 2

```
        g  4                         g  7
      f  8                         f 11
    d  3      e  5             d  4      e  7
a  1     b  2      c  3     a  2     b  2      c  5
    h  1      i  1             h  1      i  3
        j  0                         j  2
      Jan.                         Feb.


        g  8                         g  1
      f  3                         f  5
    d  5      e  7             d  6      e  8
a  3     b  2      c  5     a  4     b  2      c  6
    h  1      i  3             h  2      i  4
        j  2                         j  2
      March                        April
```

a = month digit   f = day 15 to 21
b = personal year   g = day 22 to month's end
c = a + b   h = minor attainment
d = day 1 to 7   i = minor attainment
e = day 8 to 14   j = major attainment

```
            g 3                      g 5
            f 7                      f 9
       d 7      e 9             d 8     e 1
   a 5    b 2     c 7       a 6    b 2     c 8
      h 3      i 5             h 4     i 6
            j 2                      j 2
           May                      June


            g 7                      g 9
            f 11,9                   f 4
       d 9      e 11            d 1     e 3
   a 7    b 2     c 9       a 8    b 2     c 1
      h 5      i 7             h 6     i 1
            j 2                      j 5
           July                     Aug.
```

a = month digit	f = day 15 to 21
b = personal year	g = day 22 to month's end
c = a + b	h = minor attainment
d = day 1 to 7	i = minor attainment
e = day 8 to 14	j = major attainment

g 11,9   g 4
f 22,2   f 8
d 11   e 11,2   d 3   e 5
a 9   b 2   c 11   a 1   b 2   c 3
h 7   i 0   h 1   i 1
j 7   j 0
Sept.   **Oct.**

g 22,2   g 8
f 22,6   f 3
d 11,2   e 11,4   d 5   e 7
a 11   b 2   c 11,2   a 3   b 2   c 5
h 0   i 2   h 1   i 3
j 2   j 2
Nov.   **Dec.**

a = month digit   f = day 15 to 21
b = personal year   g = day 22 to month's end
c = a + b   h = minor attainment
d = day 1 to 7   i = minor attainment
e = day 8 to 14   j = major attainment

Personal Year 3

```
        g 5                        g 7
        f 11                       f 4
    d 4      e 7              d 5      e 8
a 1     b 3     c 4       a 2     b 3     c 5
    h 2      i 1              h 1      i 2
        j 1                        j 1
        Jan.                       Feb.


        g 9                        g 11
        f 6                        f 8
    d 6      e 9              d 7      e 1
a 3     b 3     c 6       a 4     b 3     c 7
    h 0      i 3              h 1      i 4
        j 3                        j 3
       March                      April
```

a = month digit	f = day 15 to 21
b = personal year	g = day 22 to month's end
c = a + b	h = minor attainment
d = day 1 to 7	i = minor attainment
e = day 8 to 14	j = major attainment

```
          g 4                         g 6
          f 11,8                      f 3
      d 8      e 11               d 9      e 3
  a 5      b 3      c 8       a 6      b 3      c 9
      h 2      i 5               h 3      i 6
          j 3                         j 3
          May                        June


          g 8                        g 11,8
          f 5                        f 22,3
      d 1      e 4               d 11     e 11,3
  a 7      b 3      c 1       a 8      b 3      c 11
      h 4      i 2               h 5      i 1
          j 2                         j 4
          July                       Aug.
```

a = month digit   f = day 15 to 21
b = personal year   g = day 22 to month's end
c = a + b   h = minor attainment
d = day 1 to 7   i = minor attainment
e = day 8 to 14   j = major attainment

g 3
f 9
d 3   e 6
a 9   b 3   c 3
h 6   i 0
j 6
Sept.

g 5
f 11
d 4   e 7
a 1   b 3   c 4
h 2   i 1
j 1
Oct.

g 22,3
f 22,9
d 11,3   e 11,6
a 11   b 3   c 11,3
h 1   i 2
j 1
Nov.

g 9
f 6
d 6   e 9
a 3   b 3   c 6
h 0   i 3
j 3
Dec.

a = month digit   f = day 15 to 21
b = personal year   g = day 22 to month's end
c = a + b   h = minor attainment
d = day 1 to 7   i = minor attainment
e = day 8 to 14   j = major attainment

Personal Year 4

```
        g 6                      g 8
        f 5                      f 7
    d 5      e 9             d 6      e 1
a 1     b 4     c 5      a 2     b 4     c 6
    h 3      i 1             h 2      i 2
        j 2                      j 0
       Jan.                     Feb.


        g 1                      g 3
        f 11,7                   f 11
    d 7      e 11            d 8      e 3
a 3     b 4     c 7      a 4     b 4     c 8
    h 1      i 3             h 0      i 4
        j 2                      j 4
      March                    April
```

a = month digit   f = day 15 to 21
b = personal year   g = day 22 to month's end
c = a + b   h = minor attainment
d = day 1 to 7   i = minor attainment
e = day 8 to 14   j = major attainment

	g 5			g 7	
	f 4			f 6	
d 9		e 4	d 1		e 5
a 5	b 4	c 9	a 6	b 4	c 1
	h 1	i 5		h 2	i 3
	j 4			j 1	
	May			June	

	g 11,7			g 11	
	f 22,4			f 1	
d 11		e 11,4	d 3		e 7
a 7	b 4	c 11	a 8	b 1	c 3
	h 3	i 2		h 4	1 1
	j 1			j 3	
	July			Aug.	

a = month digit   f = day 15 to 21
b = personal year   g = day 22 to month's end
c = a + b   h = minor attainment
d = day 1 to 7   i = minor attainment
e = day 8 to 14   j = major attainment

```
        g 4                      g 6
        f 3                      f 5
    d 4       e 8            d 5       e 9
a 9     b 4       c 4    a 1     b 4       c 5
    h 5       i 0            h 3       i 1
        j 5                      j 2
       Sept.                    Oct.


        g 22,4                   g 1
        f 22,3                   f 11,7
   d 11,4    e 11,8          d 7       e 11
a 11   b 4      c 11,4   a 3     b 4       c 7
    h 2       i 2            h 1       i 3
        j 0                      j 2
        Nov.                    Dec.
```

a = month digit   f = day 15 to 21
b = personal year   g = day 22 to month's end
c = a + b   h = minor attainment
d = day 1 to 7   i = minor attainment
e = day 8 to 14   j = major attainment

Personal Year 5

```
        g 7_                    g 9
        f 11,6                  f 1
     d 6     e 11           d 7     e 3
  a 1    b 5    c 6      a 2    b 5    c 7
     h 4    i 1             h 3    i 2
        j 3                    j 1
       Jan.                   Feb.

        g 11                   g 4
        f 3                    f 5
     d 8     e 4            d 9     e 5
  a 3    b 5    c 8      a 4    b 5    c 9
     h 2    i 3             h 1    i 4
        j 1                    j 3
      March                  April
```

a = month digit   f = day 15 to 21
b = personal year   g = day 22 to month's end
c = a + b   h = minor attainment
d = day 1 to 7   i = minor attainment
e = day 8 to 14   j = major attainment

g 6   g 11,6
f 7   f 22,5
d 1   e 6   d 11   e 11,5
a 5   b 5   c 1   a 6   b 5   c 11
h 0   i 4   h 1   i 3
j 4   j 2
May   **June**

g 1   g 3
f 11   f 4
d 3   e 8   d 4   e 9
a 7   b 5   c 3   a 8   b 5   c 4
h 2   i 2   h 3   i 1
j 0   j 2
July   **Aug.**

a = month digit   f = day 15 to 21
b = personal year   g = day 22 to month's end
c = a + b   h = minor attainment
d = day 1 to 7   i = minor attainment
e = day 8 to 14   j = major attainment

g 5			g 7		
f 6			f 11,6		
d 5	e 1		d 6	e 11	
a 9	b 5	c 5	a 1	b 5	c 6
h 4	i 0		h 4	i 1	
j 4			j 3		
Sept.			Oct.		

g 22,5			g 11		
f 22,6			f 3		
d 11,5	e 11,1		d 8	e 4	
a 11	b 5	c 11,5	a 3	b 5	c 8
h 3	i 2		h 2	i 3	
j 1			j 1		
Nov.			Dec.		

a = month digit   f = day 15 to 21
b = personal year   g = day 22 to month's end
c = a + b   h = minor attainment
d = day 1 to 7   i = minor attainment
e = day 8 to 14   j = major attainment

Personal Year 6

```
        g 8                      g 1
        f 11                     f 4
     d 7      e 4             d 8     e 5
 a 1     b 6      c 7     a 2     b 6      c 8
     h 5      i 1             h 4     i 2
        j 4                      j 2
        Jan.                     Feb.
```

```
        g 3                      g 5
        f 6                      f 8
     d 9      e 6             d 1     e 7
 a 3     b 6      c 9     a 4     b 6      c 1
     h 3      i 3             h 2     i 5
        j 0                      j 3
       March                    April
```

a = month digit   f = day 15 to 21
b = personal year   g = day 22 to month's end
c = a + b   h = minor attainment
d = day 1 to 7   i = minor attainment
e = day 8 to 14   j = major attainment

g 11,5   g 9
f 22,6   f 3
d 11   e 11,6   d 3   e 9
a 5   b 6   c 11   a 6   b 6   c 3
h 1   i 4   h 0   i 3
j 3   j 3
May   June

g 11   g 4
f 5   f 11,5
d 4   e 1   d 5   e 11
a 7   b 6   c 4   a 8   b 6   c 5
h 1   i 2   h 2   i 1
j 1   j 1
July   Aug.

a = month digit   f = day 15 to 21
b = personal year   g = day 22 to month's end
c = a + b   h = minor attainment
d = day 1 to 7   i = minor attainment
e = day 8 to 14   j = major attainment

```
        g  6                    g  8
        f  9                    f 11
     d  6     e  3          d  7     e  4
   a 9   b 6    c 6       a 1   b 6    c 7
     h  3    i  0            h  5    i  1
        j  3                    j  4
       Sept.                   Oct.
```

```
       g 22,6                   g  3
       f 22,9                   f  6
    d 11,6   e 11,3         d  9     e  6
  a 11  b 6   c 11,6      a 3   b 6    c 9
     h  4    i  2            h  3    i  3
        j  2                    j  0
        Nov.                   Dec.
```

a = month digit   f = day 15 to 21
b = personal year   g = day 22 to month's end
c = a + b   h = minor attainment
d = day 1 to 7   i = minor attainment
e = day 8 to 14   j = major attainment

Personal Year 7

```
        g 9                          g 11
        f 5                          f 7
    d 8      e 6                  d 9      e 7
  a 1    b 7    c 8            a 2    b 7    c 9
    h 6      i 1                  h 5      i 2
        j 5                          j 3
       Jan.                         Feb.
```

```
        g 4                          g 11,4
        f 9                          f 22,7
    d 1      e 8                  d 11     e 11,7
  a 3    h 7    c 1            a 4    b 7    c 11
    h 4      i 6                  h 3      i 5
        j 2                          j 2
      March                        April
```

a = month digit   f = day 15 to 21
b = personal year   g = day 22 to month's end
c = a + b   h = minor attainment
d = day 1 to 7   i = minor attainment
e = day 8 to 14   j = major attainment

g 8
f 4
d 3   e 1
a 5   b 7   c 3
h 2   i 4
j 2
May

g 1
f 11,4
d 4   e 11
a 6   b 7   c 4
h 1   i 3
j 2
June

g 3
f 8
d 5   e 3
a 7   b 7   c 5
h 0   i 2
j 2
July

g 5
f 1
d 6   e 4
a 8   b 7   c 6
h 1   i 1
j 0
Aug.

a = month digit   f = day 15 to 21
b = personal year   g = day 22 to month's end
c = a + b   h = minor attainment
d = day 1 to 7   i = minor attainment
e = day 8 to 14   j = major attainment

	g 7	
	f 3	
d 7		e 5
a 9	b 7	c 7
h 2		i 0
	j 2	
	Sept.	

	g 9	
	f 5	
d 8		e 6
a 1	b 7	c 8
h 6		i 1
	j 5	
	Oct.	

	g 22,7	
	f 22,3	
d 11,7		e 11,5
a 11	b 7	c 11,7
h 5		i 2
	j 3	
	Nov.	

	g 4	
	f 9	
d 1		e 8
a 3	b 7	c 1
h 4		i 6
	j 2	
	Dec.	

a = month digit

b = personal year

c = a + b

d = day 1 to 7

e = day 8 to 14

f = day 15 to 21

g = day 22 to month's end

h = minor attainment

i = minor attainment

j = major attainment

Personal Year 8

```
        g 1                          g 3
        f 8                          f 1
   d 9       e 8                 d 1       e 9
 a 1    b 8    c 9             a 2    b 8    c 1
   h 7       i 1                 h 6       i 7
        j 6                          j 1
        Jan.                         Feb.
```

```
        g 11,3                       g 7
        f 22,8                       f 11,3
   d 11      e 11,8              d 3       e 11
 a 3    b 8    c 11            a 4    b 8    c 3
   h 5       i 6                 h 4       i 5
        j 1                          j 1
       March                        April
```

a = month digit   f = day 15 to 21
b = personal year   g = day 22 to month's end
c = a + b   h = minor attainment
d = day 1 to 7   i = minor attainment
e = day 8 to 14   j = major attainment

```
        g 9                    g 11
        f 7                    f 9
    d 4     e 3            d 5     e 4
a 5     b 8     c 4    a 6     b 8     c 5
    h 3     i 4            h 2     i 3
        j 1                    j 1
        May                   June


        g 4                    g 6
        f 11                   f 4
    d 6     e 5            d 7     e 6
a 7     b 8     c 6    a 8     b 8     c 7
    h 1     i 2            h 0     i 1
        j 1                    j 1
        July                  Aug.
```

a = month digit   f = day 15 to 21
b = personal year   g = day 22 to month's end
c = a + b   h = minor attainment
d = day 1 to 7   i = minor attainment
e = day 8 to 14   j = major attainment

	g 8				g 1	
	f 6				f 8	
	d 8	e 7			d 9	e 8
a 9	b 8	c 8		a 1	b 8	c 9
	h 1	i 0			h 7	i 1
	j 1				j 6	
	Sept.				Oct.	

	g 22,8				g 11,3	
	f 22,6				f 22,8	
	d 11,8	e 11,7			d 11	e 11,8
a 11	b 8	c 11,8		a 3	b 8	c 11
	h 6	i 7			h 5	i 6
	j 1				j 1	
	Nov.				Dec.	

a = month digit   f = day 15 to 21
b = personal year   g = day 22 to month's end
c = a + b   h = minor attainment
d = day 1 to 7   i = minor attainment
e = day 8 to 14   j = major attainment

Personal Year 9

```
        g  2                      g 11,2
        f  2                      f 22,9
     d  1      e  1            d 11      e 11,9
 a 1     b 9      c 1       a 2     b 9      c 11
     h  8      i  8            h  7      i  7
        j  0                      j  0
        Jan.                      Feb.
```

```
        g  6                      g  8
        f  6                      f  8
     d  3      e  3            d  4      e  4
 a 3     b 9      c 3       a 4     b 9      c 4
     h  6      i  6            h  5      i  5
        j  0                      j  0
       March                     April
```

a = month digit   f = day 15 to 21
b = personal year   g = day 22 to month's end
c = a + b   h = minor attainment
d = day 1 to 7   i = minor attainment
e = day 8 to 14   j = major attainment

```
              g 1                              g 3
              f 1                              f 3
        d 5      e 5                     d 6      e 6
   a 5     b 9      c 5              a 6     b 9      c 6
        h 4      i 4                     h 3      i 3
              j 0                              j 0
              May                             June


              g 5                              g 7
              f 5                              f 7
        d 7      e 7                     d 8      e 8
   a 7     b 9      c 7              a 8     b 9      c 8
        h 2      i 2                     h 1      i 1
              j 0                              j 0
             July                             Aug.
```

a = month digit   f = day 15 to 21
b = personal year   g = day 22 to month's end
c = a + b   h = minor attainment
d = day 1 to 7   i = minor attainment
e = day 8 to 14   j = major attainment

g 9
f 9
d 9   e 9
a 9   b 9   c 9
h 0   i 0
j 0
Sept.

g 2
f 2
d 1   e 1
a 1   b 9   c 1
h 8   i 8
j 0
Oct.

g 22,9
f 22,9
d 11,9   e 11,9
a 11   b 9   c 11,9
h 7   i 7
j 0
Nov.

g 6
f 6
d 3   e 3
a 3   b 9   c 3
h 6   i 6
j 0
Dec.

a = month digit
b = personal year
c = a + b
d = day 1 to 7
e = day 8 to 14
f = day 15 to 21
g = day 22 to month's end
h = minor attainment
i = minor attainment
j = major attainment

Personal Year 11

g 11,2
f 33,2
d 11,1   e 22,1
a 1   b 11   c 11,1
h 1   i 1
j 0
Jan.

g 11,4
f 33,4
d 11,2   e 22,2
a 2   b 11   c 11,2
h 0   i 2
j 2
Feb.

g 11,6
f 33,6
d 11,3   e 22,3
a 3   b 11   c 11,3
h 1   i 3
j 2
March

g 11,8
f 33,8
d 11,4   e 22,4
a 4   b 11   c 11,4
h 2   i 4
j 2
April

a = month digit   f = day 15 to 21
b = personal year   g = day 22 to month's end
c = a + b   h = minor attainment
d = day 1 to 7   i = minor attainment
e = day 8 to 14   j = major attainment

	g 11,1			g 11,3	
	f 33,1			f 33,3	
d 11,5	e 22,5		d 11,6	e 22,6	
a 5	b 11	c 11,5	a 6	b 11	c 11,6
h 3	i 5		h 4	i 6	
	j 2			j 2	
	May			June	

	g 11,5			g 11,7	
	f 33,5			f 33,7	
d 11,7	e 22,7		d 11,8	e 22,8	
a 7	b 11	c 11,7	a 8	b 11	c 11,8
h 5	i 7		h 6	i 1	
	j 2			j 5	
	July			Aug.	

a = month digit
b = personal year
c = a + b
d = day 1 to 7
e = day 8 to 14

f = day 15 to 21
g = day 22 to month's end
h = minor attainment
i = minor attainment
j = major attainment

g 11,9   g 11,2
f 33,9   f 33,2
d 11,9   e 22,9   d 11,1   e 22,1
a 9   b 11   c 11,9   a 1   b 11   c 11,1
h 7   i 0   h 1   i 1
j 7   j 0
Sept.   Oct.

g 33   g 11,6
f 55   f 33,6
d 22   e 33   d 11,3   e 22,3
a 11   b 11   c 22   a 3   b 11   c 11,3
h 0   i 11   h 1   i 3
j 11   j 2
Nov.   Dec.

a = month digit   f = day 15 to 21
b = personal year   g = day 22 to month's end
c = a + b   h = minor attainment
d = day 1 to 7   i = minor attainment
e = day 8 to 14   j = major attainment

Personal Year 22

g 22,2   g 22,4
f 66,2   f 66,4
d 22,1 e 44,1   d 22,2 e 44,2
a 1   b 22   c 22,1   a 2   b 22   c 22,2
h 3   i 1   h 2   i 2
j 2   j 0
Jan.   Feb.

g 22,6   g 22,8
f 66,6   f 66,8
d 22,3 e 44,3   d 22,4 e 44,4
a 3   b 22   c 22,3   a 4   b 22   c 22,4
h 1   i 3   h 0   i 4
j 2   j 4
March   April

a = month digit   f = day 15 to 21
b = personal year   g = day 22 to month's end
c = a + b   h = minor attainment
d = day 1 to 7   i = minor attainment
e = day 8 to 14   j = major attainment

g 22,1
f 66,1
d 22,5   e 44,5
a 5   b 22   c 22,5
h 1   i 5
j 4
May

g 22,3
f 66,3
d 22,6   e 44,6
a 6   b 22   c 22,6
h 2   i 3
j 1
June

g 22,5
f 66,5
d 22,7   e 44,7
a 7   b 22   c 22,7
h 3   i 2
j 1
July

g 22,7
f 66,7
d 22,8   e 44,8
a 8   b 22   c 22,8
h 4   i 1
j 3
Aug.

a = month digit   f = day 15 to 21
b = personal year   g = day 22 to month's end
c = a + b   h = minor attainment
d = day 1 to 7   i = minor attainment
e = day 8 to 14   j = major attainment

g 22,9
f 66,9
d 22,9   e 44,9
a 9   b 22   c 22,9
h 5   i 0
j 5
Sept.

g 22,2
f 66,2
d 22,1   e 44,1
a 1   b 22   c 22,1
h 3   i 1
j 2
Oct.

g 44
f 88
d 33   e 55
a 11   b 22   c 33
h 11   i 11
j 0
Nov.

g 22,6
f 66,6
d 22,3   e 44,3
a 3   b 22   c 22,3
h 1   i 3
j 2
Dec.

a = month digit
b = personal year
c = a + b
d = day 1 to 7
e = day 8 to 14
f = day 15 to 21
g = day 22 to month's end
h = minor attainment
i = minor attainment
j = major attainment

❧ Appendix B ❧

A Blank Chart for Personal Use

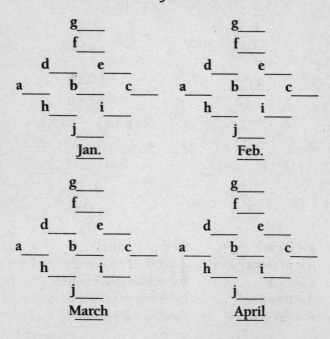

g____
f____

d____   e____

a____   b____   c____

h____   i____

j____

Jan.

g____
f____

d____   e____

a____   b____   c____

h____   i____

j____

Feb.

g____
f____

d____   e____

a____   b____   c____

h____   i____

j____

March

g____
f____

d____   e____

a____   b____   c____

h____   i____

j____

April

a = month digit   f = day 15 to 21
b = personal year   g = day 22 to month's end
c = a + b   h = minor attainment
d = day 1 to 7   i = minor attainment
e = day 8 to 14   j = major attainment

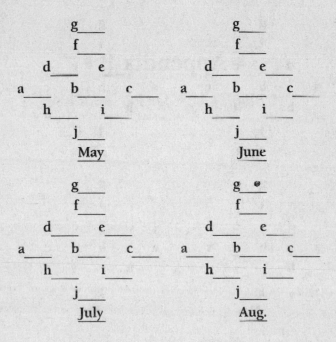

```
        g____                          g____
        f___                           f___
    d___      e___                  d___      e___
a___     b___     c___          a___     b___     c___
    h___      i___                  h___      i___
        j___                            j___
        May                            June


        g____                          g  ●
        f___                           f___
    d___      e___                  d___      e___
a___     b___     c___          a___     b___     c___
    h___      i___                  h___      i___
        j___                            j___
        July                           Aug.
```

a = month digit   f = day 15 to 21
b = personal year   g = day 22 to month's end
c = a + b   h = minor attainment
d = day 1 to 7   i = minor attainment
e = day 8 to 14   j = major attainment

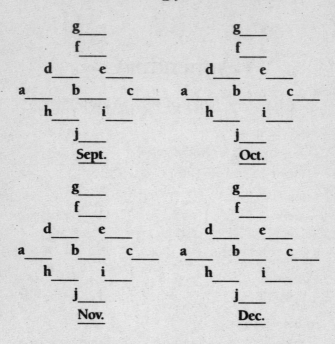

a = month digit   f = day 15 to 21
b = personal year   g = day 22 to month's end
c = a + b   h = minor attainment
d = day 1 to 7   i = minor attainment
e = day 8 to 14   j = major attainment

❧ Appendix C ❧

Characteristics of the Attainments

Attainment 0
1. No problems 2. Nothing new
3. No specific attainment

Attainment 1
1. Work 2. A change in a position 3. A new beginning
4. Leadership 5. Independence 6. Aloneness

Attainment 2
1. Dependence 2. Double 3. Affection
4. Following 5. Lack of money 6. Subservience

Attainment 3
1. Friends 2. Social situations 3. Pleasantness
4. Children 5. Pets 6. Creativity 7. Happiness

Attainment 4
1. Work 2. Restriction 3. Hardness 4. Dependability
5. Sturdiness

Attainment 5
1. Change 2. Temporary
3. Attraction to opposite sex 4. Parties 5. Travel

Attainment 6

1. Love 2. Home 3. Family 4. Health or illness
5. Good looks 6. Hearing 7. Confidence

Attainment 7

1. Unexpected 2. Delay 3. Aloneness 4. Teaching
5. Religion 6. Science and research 7. By chance

Attainment 8

1. Work 2. Authority 3. Power 4. Material things
5. Money

Attainment 9

1. Travel 2. Teaching 3. Endings or beginnings
4. Humanitarian pursuits 5. Kindness

Attainment 11

1. Religion 2. Inspiration 3. Limelight 4. Theater
5. Aviation 6.Psychic ability 7. Relating to God

Attainment 22

1. Work 2. Humanitarian position 3. Group
4. Dominance

❦ Glossary ❦

Attainments

The **attainments** are what can be achieved or attained under the vibrations of a particular month. The **attainments** for each month are found in the bottom triangle of the numerology chart for finding work.

Compound Numbers

Compound numbers are the combination of the main nine numbers and masters numbers—or the combination of master numbers with other master numbers. **Compound numbers** are written with commas between the elements of the number to show all the elements of the number. **Compound numbers** are formed because master numbers are not broken down. Examples of compound numbers are **(11,2)**, **(11,5)**, **(22,1)**, **(22,3)**, or **(22,6)**.

Day Digit

The **day digit** is the date of a day reduced, as far as it can be, in numerology terms. A **day digit** may be one of the main nine numbers or it may be a master number.

Descriptor Numbers

Descriptor numbers are numbers that are not work numbers by themselves, but can help describe a work number, a work vibration, a work situation, or the vibration of a time period. The main **descriptor numbers** are 2, 3, 5, 6, 7, 9, and 11. **Descriptor numbers** can be simple numbers or part of a compound number.

Main Nine Numbers

The **main nine numbers** in numerology are the numbers 1 to 9. These numbers represent different vibrations that correspond to characteristics of a day, or to what may possibly happen during a period of time.

Master Numbers

The **master numbers** are 11, 22, and 33 and other numbers in this form that are composed of the same double digit. These are numbers that represent a more intense vibration than the vibrations of the main nine numbers. The **master numbers** have the characteristic of standing alone. That means that they are not broken down and added to other numbers. They may be combined with other numbers, but are not usually reduced. Sometimes to simplify understanding they might be reduced.

Month Digit

The **month digit** is the numerological number for the month. It is the number of the month reduced as far as possible. Use the following table for the **month digits.** The month of November is the only one that is a little complicated. The 11 of the number for November should also be checked as a 2, because often 11 is being lived at its lower vibration of 2.

The table that follows will show the month digit for each month.

January = 1	July = 7
February = 2	August = 8
March = 3	September = 9
April = 4	October = 10 = (1+0) = 1
May = 5	November = 11 = (1+1) = 2
	or 11 (master number)
June = 6	December = 12 = (1+2) = 3

Numerology

Numerology is a means of using numbers to depict vibrations. **Numerology** comes from the teachings and calculations of the Greek philosopher, Pythagoras, creator of the Pythagorean theorem. **Numerology** can be used to show the vibrations of people, the vibrations of a time period, or the vibrations of a person within a time period.

Personal Year

The **personal year** is the numerological number for how a year will affect a person individually. To find the **personal year**, first find the universal year and add it to one's month and day of birth. The month and day of birth should already be reduced as far as possible.

Simple Numbers

Simple numbers are the main nine numbers as they stand alone, or the master numbers as they stand alone.

Universal Year

The **universal year** is the numerological number for a particular year. It is found by adding together the digits of a year and then numerologically reducing them as far as possible. Everyone is under the same **universal year.**

Vibrations

Vibrations are energy patterns. There are **vibrations** of people, **vibrations** of time periods, and **vibrations** of people within time periods. Energy **vibrations** are one of the building blocks of the universe and can be expressed in numeric form through numerology.

Week Digit

The **week digit** is the numerological number for the vibration of a specific week. It may be one of the main nine numbers, a master number, or a compound number.

To find the **week digit** of the first 7 days of the month, add together the month digit and the personal year in the numerological chart for job hunting. To find the second week (the **8th** to the **14th**) add together the personal year and third number in the base line of a numerology chart for job hunting. To find the third week (the **15th** to the **21st,** including the **21st**) add together the week digits for week **1** and week **2.** To find the last part of the month, which is usually over a week (the **22nd** to the end of the month), add together the month digit and the third number in the base line.

Work Numbers

Work numbers are those numbers under whose vibration it is a good time to look for work. The main **work numbers** are **1, 4, 8,** and **22. Work numbers** also include any simple or compound number that has one of the main **work numbers** in it—or that, if broken down, add up to a **work number.** This is because both these types of numbers will have some of the characteristics of a main **work number.**

Included in this group are numbers such as **13, 14, 17, 18, 19, 24, 26, 28,** and **31** (all simple numbers found in the calendar). Also included are numbers like **(2,11), (4,11), (6,11), (8,11), (11,11)** (all forms of **22**) and other compounds in the same pattern.

❧ Bibliography ❧

Avery, Kevin Quinn, D.Ms.. *The Numbers of Life*. Garden City, New York: Doubleday & Company, Inc., 1977.

Bishop, Barbara J.. *Numerology: Universal Vibrations of Numbers*. St. Paul, MN: Llewellyn, 1990.

Hitchcock, Helen. *Helping Yourself With Numerology*. Englewood Cliffs, NJ: Prentice Hall, 1986.

Mykian, W.. *Numerology Made Easy*. Hollywood, CA: Wilshire Book Company, 1979.

Taylor, Ariel Yvon. *Numerology Made Plain*. Van Nuys, CA: Newcastle Publishing Company, 1973.

Stay in Touch. . .Llewellyn publishes hundreds of books on your favorite subject

On the following pages you will find some books now available on related subjects. Your local bookstore stocks most of these and will stock new Llewellyn titles as they become available. We urge your patronage.

Order by Phone
Call toll-free within the U.S. and Canada, **1–800–THE MOON.**.
In Minnesota call **(612) 291–1970**.
We accept Visa, MasterCard, and American Express.

Order by Mail
Send the full price of your order (MN residents add 7% sales tax) in U.S. funds to:

Llewellyn Worldwide
P.O. Box 64383, Dept. K 039–6
St. Paul, MN 55164–0383, U.S.A.

Postage and Handling
- ◆ $4.00 for orders $15.00 and under
- ◆ $5.00 for orders over $15.00
- ◆ No charge for orders over $100.00

We ship UPS in the continental United States. We cannot ship to P.O. boxes. Orders shipped to Alaska, Hawaii, Canada, Mexico, and Puerto Rico will be sent first-class mail.

International orders: Airmail—add freight equal to price of each book to the total price of order, plus $5.00 for each non-book item (audiotapes, etc.). Surface mail—Add $1.00 per item. Allow 4–6 weeks delivery on all orders. Postage and handling rates subject to change.

Group Discounts
We offer a 20% quantity discount to group leaders or agents. You must order a minimum of 5 copies of the same book to get our special quantity price.

Free Catalog

Get a free copy of our color catalog, *New Worlds of Mind and Spirit*. Subscribe for just $10.00 in the United States and Canada ($20.00 overseas, first class mail). Many bookstores carry *New Worlds*—ask for it!